# DROID Application
# Sketch Book

**Dean Kaplan**

Apress®

**DROID Application Sketch Book**

ISBN-13 (pbk): 978-1-4302-3358-9

Printed and bound in the United States of America 9 8 7 6 5 4 3 2 1

President and Publisher: Paul Manning
Editorial Board: Steve Anglin, Mark Beckner, Ewan Buckingham, Gary Cornell, Jonathan Gennick, Jonathan Hassell, Michelle Lowman, Matthew Moodie, Duncan Parkes, Jeffrey Pepper, Frank Pohlmann, Douglas Pundick, Ben Renow-Clarke, Dominic Shakeshaft, Matt Wade, Tom Welsh
Compositor: Apress Production
Cover Designer: Anna Ishchenko

Distributed to the book trade worldwide by Springer Science+Business Media, LLC., 233 Spring Street, 6th Floor, New York, NY 10013. Phone 1-800-SPRINGER, fax (201) 348-4505, e-mail orders-ny@springer-sbm.com, or visit www.springeronline.com.

For information on translations, please e-mail rights@apress.com, or visit www.apress.com.

Apress and friends of ED books may be purchased in bulk for academic, corporate, or promotional use. eBook versions and licenses are also available for most titles. For more information, reference our Special Bulk Sales–eBook Licensing web page at www.apress.com/info/bulksales.

The information in this book is distributed on an "as is" basis, without warranty. Although every precaution has been taken in the preparation of this work, neither the author(s) nor Apress shall have any liability to any person or entity with respect to any loss or damage caused or alleged to be caused directly or indirectly by the information contained in this work.

# Introduction

The *DROID Application Sketch Book* is the brainchild of Dean Kaplan who understood the need of smartphone application designers for a place to sketch and keep sketches of their design ideas. He has taken this idea and transferred it to the DROID. With the knowledge that people often write their ideas on a whiteboard, only to lose them or other important details later, we created a sketchbook appropriate for the various versions of DROID.

The idea, of course, is really simple. Give the user 150 pages of grid space to draw or layout their plans, sketches or whatever, for their DROID applications. Users have found a number of unexpected uses for the book.

The book features:

- A grid background on each page.
- A lay flat binding so that you can have a hand on your DROID and one on a pencil.
- 150 pages to write, draw, compose or doodle on.
- An organized place for your user interface designs.
- Perforations so that you can take the pages out if you wish.

To use the lay flat binding, simply open the book to the page you wish and in the gutter crease both pages with your hand. To tear out a page it is a good idea to fold the page on the perforation and crease it before tearing.

We hope that you will find the book useful for whatever purpose you choose.

# About the Author

Dean Kaplan is founder and owner of Kapsoft, a technology consulting firm specializing in software applications for engineering applications. Kapsoft provides a full spectrum of product design and development services including manufacturing automation, cellular and location services, material handling, automatic identification, network analysis and protocols, telecommunications, telecom billing, healthcare, and bond trading. Dean recently designed and executed a new synthetic instrument product serving as a replacement for five or more legacy RF test instruments.

Dean anticipated a need for simple effective smartphone design tools and created Application Sketch Books for the iPhone and the iPAD to fill that void. Kapsoft is currently deeply involved in new exciting accessory development for the various smartphone platforms. More information about other related Kapsoft smartphone products may be obtained at MobileSketchBook.com.

Dean Kaplan was born in Philadelphia and to this day still resides in nearby Haverford, Pennsylvania. Dean has a Bachelor of Science in Electrical Engineering Technology obtained from Temple University in 1982. Dean writes a contemporary technology blog at DeanOnSoftware.com. For info about Kapsoft, please see Kapsoft.com. You can also follow Dean on Twitter at @Kapsoft.

Application Name:

Screen Name:

Application Name: _____

Screen Name: _____

Application Name:

Screen Name:

Application Name:

Screen Name:

Application Name:

Screen Name: